THE MICROWAVE
Shakespeare

Other titles in the series

Hamlet
Macbeth
The Merchant of Venice
A Midsummer Night's Dream
Much Ado About Nothing
Romeo and Juliet
The Tempest
Twelfth Night

THE TRAGEDY OF JULIUS CAESAR

Jill Atkins

Illustrated by Daisy Hawkins

Julius Caesar
Published by Ransom Publishing Ltd.
Unit 7, Brocklands Farm, West Meon, Hampshire GU32 1JN, UK
www.ransom.co.uk

ISBN   978 178591 637 3
First published in 2019

Copyright © 2019 Ransom Publishing Ltd.
Text copyright © 2019 Ransom Publishing Ltd.
Cover illustration copyright © wynnter
Illustrations copyright © Daisy Hawkins; Flannymagic; chrupka. Globe theatre today: claudiodivizia. Original Globe theatre illustration: C. Walter Hodges, licensed under the Creative Commons Attribution-Share Alike 4.0 International (https://creativecommons.org/licenses/by-sa/4.0/deed.en) license.

A CIP catalogue record of this book is available from the British Library.

All rights reserved. No part of this publication may be reproduced, stored in a retrieval system, or transmitted, in any form or by any means, electronic, mechanical, photocopying, recording or otherwise, without the prior permission of the publishers.

The rights of Jill Atkins to be identified as the author and of Daisy Hawkins to be identified as the illustrator of this Work have been asserted by them in accordance with sections 77 and 78 of the Copyright, Design and Patents Act 1988.

CONTENTS

Where	6
When	7
Who	8
The Globe Theatre	11
One	12
Two	21
Three	28
Four	41
Five	46
What's the play about?	52
What are the main themes in the play?	54
Shakespeare's words	58

WHERE

In the ancient city of Rome, in Italy, and on the plains of Philippi (which is in modern-day Greece).

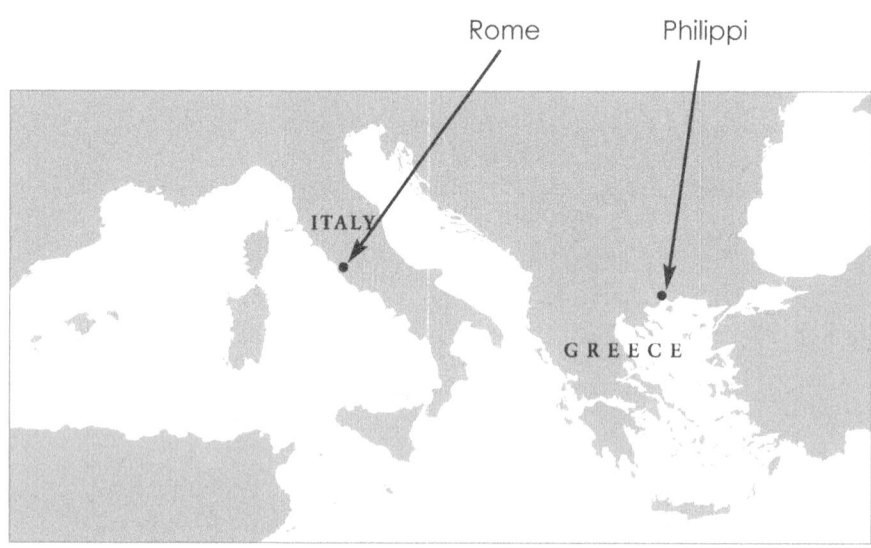

WHEN

The play was written in 1599.

The action takes place between 44 and 42 BCE.

The full title of the play is *The Tragedy of Julius Caesar*.

The play is based on true events from Roman history. Most of the characters in the play – including Julius Caesar, Brutus and Cassius – were real people.

Julius Caesar was assassinated in 44 BCE.

HELPFUL NOTE

All the spoken words in this book that are in italics, '*like this*', are actual words taken from Shakespeare's play. They are spoken by one of the actors in the play.

WHO

Julius Caesar – Emperor of Rome

Brutus (also called **Marcus Brutus**)
– senator and conspirator

Cassius – senator and conspirator

Julius Caesar   Brutus   Cassius

Antony (also called **Mark Antony**) – Caesar's favourite

Octavius Caesar – great nephew and adopted son of Julius Caesar

Antony   Octavius Caesar

Casca – senator and conspirator

Cinna – senator and conspirator

Decius Brutus – senator and conspirator

Metellus Cimber – senator and conspirator

Cicero – a senator

Lepidus – friend of Octavius and Antony

Calpurnia – wife of Julius Caesar

Portia – wife of Brutus

Flavius – a tribune (a kind of officer)

Marullus – a tribune

Artemidorus – a teacher

Cinna – a poet

soothsayer

Messala – a soldier

The Globe Theatre. Above is a reconstruction of the original Globe Theatre, which is in London. Below is a cross-section of the original theatre, which was built in 1599.

Shakespeare's plays were performed at this theatre. When you read this book, just imagine standing in the crowd, in front of this stage, watching the play.

ONE

We are on the streets in Rome, Italy, in the year 44 BCE. A big crowd has gathered and there is great excitement in the air. Amongst the crowd are two tribunes (or officers), **Flavius** and **Marullus**. They're talking to a carpenter and a cobbler.

Flavius asks them why they have stopped work. The cobbler tells him, 'S*ir, we make holiday,*

to see Caesar and to rejoice in his triumph.'

(Julius Caesar's old rival was the Roman statesman and general Pompey, who is long dead. Caesar has just defeated Pompey's sons in battle. That's the '*triumph*' that everybody's excited about.)

Marullus isn't impressed. '*Wherefore rejoice? What conquest brings he home?*' he asks. 'What foreign lands has Caesar conquered? What victory does he bring home? None! He's just been fighting other Romans. *You blocks, you stones, you worse than senseless things!* Didn't you know Pompey?'

Marullus reminds the men how they used to cheer for Pompey, in the same way that they now do for Caesar. 'And now you strew flowers in Caesar's path, as he comes in triumph over Pompey's defeated sons.'

Flavius tells the men to go home.

When the crowd has moved on, Flavius and Marullus pull down the decorations from the statues of Julius Caesar.

'If we take away these decorations supporting Caesar,' says Flavius, 'maybe it will make Caesar come back down to Earth.'

Flavius and Marullus definitely aren't fans of Caesar, then!

In another part of Rome, there is a fanfare of trumpets and **Caesar** enters. He is followed by a large number of important senators: **Brutus, Antony, Cassius, Casca, Decius Brutus** and **Cicero**.

Caesar's wife **Calpurnia** and Brutus' wife **Portia** are there, too.

A large crowd follows behind them. Caesar is soaking up all this attention. He loves it! He thinks he's a big celebrity.

Suddenly a **soothsayer** steps forward from the crowd. He says he can see into the future. He calls out to Caesar, '*Beware the ides of March.*' (That's the Roman way of saying 15th March.)

Caesar ignores the soothsayer and sends him away. Then he carries on walking along the street.

Only Brutus and Cassius stay where they are. They are talking in hushed voices. Cassius tells Brutus he's noticed that Brutus has been rather quiet lately.

'It's nothing,' says Brutus. 'I've been troubled with private thoughts recently. Nothing to worry about.'

'It's a pity you can't see your own worth,' replies Cassius. 'I've heard a lot of the noblest Romans speaking well of you – and complaining about our current leader.'

Is Cassius hinting that Brutus could be leader instead of Caesar? Brutus says he won't listen to such dangerous talk.

They hear shouting in the distance.

'*I do fear, the people*
Choose Caesar for their king,' says Brutus.
(Roman leaders were called 'emperors'.
Crowning Caesar 'king' would be a new
thing, giving him much more power.)

'Aha!' says Cassius. '*Then must I think
you would not have it so.*'

Cassius doesn't leave it there. He is
jealous that Caesar has risen so far. 'I'd
rather not live at all than live to worship a
man who's just like me. *I was born free as
Caesar; so were you.* What's so special
about him?' Cassius asks. 'He's no better
than me.'

Cassius tells Brutus about how he once
rescued Caesar from a river – '*And this man
Is now become a god, and Cassius is
A wretched creature …* '

There is another shout, followed by
trumpets. More praise for Caesar.

Cassius is angry and bitter. '*Why, man, he
doth bestride the narrow world
Like a Colossus, and we petty men*

*Walk under his huge legs and peep about
To find ourselves dishonourable graves.'*

Cassius says again that Brutus is miles better than Caesar. Brutus begs Cassius to say nothing more for the time being.

Caesar returns, followed as usual by everybody else. Brutus notices that Caesar looks angry; he wonders what's been happening.

Caesar beckons to Antony, who is his favourite. Caesar has noticed Cassius and can see that he's not happy.

*'Yond Cassius has a lean and hungry look;
He thinks too much: such men are dangerous,'*
Caesar tells Antony.

Antony tells him not to worry, but Caesar goes on. 'If I was going to be afraid of anybody, it would be Cassius. He reads a lot, he watches people and he rarely smiles. Such men are hardly ever happy if there is somebody greater than themselves. He is very dangerous.' (Well spotted, Caesar!)

Then Caesar and most of his followers

leave. Brutus, Cassius and Casca are left standing there.

'What was all that shouting about?' asks Brutus.

'Antony offered to make Caesar king three times and each time Caesar refused it,' replies Casca. 'Then Caesar had a fainting fit – but the crowd still shouted for him. There's other news, too,' Casca tells Cassius. 'Flavius and Marullus have been *put to silence*, just for pulling down the decorations.'

Brutus and Casca leave, and Cassius is left talking to himself. 'Caesar doesn't like me, but he loves Brutus. Tonight I'll send Brutus some letters of support in different handwriting. Because we need to remove Caesar – or we'll suffer even worse than we are suffering now.'

Later in the day, a storm is raging as Casca meets up with Cicero in another street in

Rome. Casca's very jumpy; he's never seen such a storm. Weird things have been happening, too. He thinks they are an omen of bad things to come.

Cicero asks Casca if Caesar is going to the Capitol tomorrow. (The Capitol is where all the senators meet.) Casca tells him that he is.

Cicero has just left when Cassius arrives. He loves the storm; he's excited by the violence of the thunder and lightning. Casca says he hates it, but Cassius tells him he's dull. 'Right now, Casca, I could name a man who is just like this storm, *that thunders, lightens, opens graves, and roars*, just like the lion in the Capitol.' (He means Caesar).

'*They say the senators tomorrow*

Mean to establish Caesar as a king,' Casca tells Cassius.

That's the last thing Cassius wants! He warns Casca, '*I know where I will wear this dagger then.*' He plans to put an end to Caesar. 'Are you with me?' he asks.

19

Casca says he is. They agree to keep quiet about it for the time being. Cassius knows other people who feel the same way as him, and they're waiting for him now.

'The sky tonight looks like the work we have to do: *Most bloody, fiery, and most terrible,*' Cassius tells Casca.

Everyone's out and about in the storm. Then **Cinna** turns up. He's in on the plot too. He tells Cassius, '*O Cassius, if you could
But win the noble Brutus to our party.*'

That's exactly what Cassius aims to do. Everyone likes and respects good old Brutus; he's 'mister nice guy'. If they get him on board, it'll all be a lot easier.

Cassius gives Cinna a letter of support to throw in at Brutus's window.

Then, even though it's midnight, Cassius and Casca set off for Brutus's house. They need to get him on their side before morning.

TWO

At Brutus's house it is well past midnight. Brutus can't sleep; he is pacing the floor, worrying about what to do about Caesar.

'*It must be by his death,*' he thinks. 'Will crowning Caesar as king change him? Yes,' he thinks, 'it will. If we crown him king, *then, I grant, we put a sting in him*

That at his will he may do danger with.'

We must treat Caesar as if he was a serpent's [snake's] egg, Brutus says. When hatched it can do great damage – so we must kill it before it hatches.

Then Brutus's servant brings him a letter

that he found by the window. Brutus asks the servant, '*Is not to-morrow, boy, the ides of March?*' It is. Brutus remembers what the soothsayer said to Caesar.

By the light of the candle, Brutus reads the letter. It's from Cassius, pleading with him to join them in their plan.

What should Brutus do?

At that moment, there's knocking at the gate. It's Cassius and others. Their hats are pulled down and their faces are hidden by cloaks. Very shady! Brutus invites them in.

Brutus recognises the other men and he knows what they have come for. They all shake hands. Cassius wants them all to '*swear our resolution*' (to kill Caesar). But Brutus says they don't need to swear an oath; their cause is good, and that's enough.

They talk about Cicero. Should they ask him to join them? He's old and wise. 'No,' says Brutus. '*For he will never follow anything*

That other men begin.'

They decide to leave him out.

Will they murder only Caesar? Or should they kill Antony, too? He's Caesar's favourite, after all.

'No,' says Brutus. '*Our course will seem too bloody …*

To cut the head off and then hack the limbs

… For Antony is but a limb of Caesar.'

Is Brutus making a big mistake? Cassius thinks so. But in the end it's agreed: Antony will not be killed.

The clock strikes three. Soon it will be

light. Cassius wonders whether Caesar will go out in public today. He's very superstitious and, after all, today *is* the Ides of March! Decius Brutus promises to talk Caesar round. 'I will bring him to the Capitol,' he says.

It's almost morning and Brutus sends everyone away. He tells them to look cheerful. 'Put on an act. Don't let anyone suspect us.'

He's just seeing everyone out when his wife, Portia, comes to fetch him to bed. She says he's been acting out of character lately. What's bothering him?

He says he's feeling fine, but she knows him too well. '*No, my Brutus;*

You have some sick offence within your mind,

Which, by the right and virtue of my place,

I ought to know of.' She begs him to tell her what's wrong. '*I grant I am a woman; but withal*

A woman that Lord Brutus took to wife.'

Brutus is torn. He knows he can trust her. But should he tell her what's going on?

Then, just before he can say anything, there's another knock at the door. It's somebody else who has promised to support Brutus.

Things are stacking up against Caesar.

Meanwhile, at Caesar's house, Caesar is also having trouble sleeping. It's early morning now, but the storm is still raging.

Caesar's wife Calpurnia tries to persuade him not to leave the house. She's heard lots of rumours of weird things happening in the streets. 'Even graves have cracked open and *yielded up their dead.*' She says it's all a warning.

'It's safe,' says Caesar. 'These bad omens apply to the world as a whole, and not just to me.' But he agrees to stay at home for the day; Mark Antony will tell people he's not well.

But, just in the nick of time, Decius Brutus arrives. He's very upbeat. He's come to take Caesar to the Capitol.

Caesar tells him he's not going.

When Decius Brutus demands a real reason (not just illness), Caesar blames his wife. He says Calpurnia has had nightmares and fears for her husband's safety.

But Decius Brutus is clever; he teases Caesar and mentions that today is the day the senate was going to crown him king.

Caesar changes his mind like a shot. He's going!

At that moment, Brutus and the other conspirators arrive at Caesar's home. So they all set out for the Capitol together. But it doesn't stop Brutus feeling bad about what they are going to do. He's got a guilty conscience before he's even done anything!

In a street near the Capitol, **Artemidorus**, a teacher, stands waiting for Caesar. He has written a letter. It names all the conspirators and warns Caesar not to trust any of them. He wants to hand the letter to Caesar before he gets to the Capitol.

Has there been a leak?

A bit further along the street, Portia is waiting outside her house. She's really worried about Brutus, so she sends her servant to check on him.

'Come back and tell me if your master looks well. And keep an eye on Caesar. Tell me what he does.'

Then a soothsayer hurries along the street. Portia asks him if he can forsee anything about Caesar. Is any harm intended towards Caesar today?

'Nothing that I know for sure,' says the soothsayer, 'but much that I fear might happen.'

THREE

In a street in front of the Capitol, a crowd has gathered. Caesar arrives, followed by the usual important people.

Caesar sees the soothsayer and tells him that the ides of March have come.

'*Ay, Caesar; but not gone,*' replies the soothsayer.

Then Artemidorus steps forward with his letter. He asks Caesar to read it, but Decius Brutus distracts Caesar with something else to read.

Caesar then goes up to the Senate House and everybody follows him, leaving just

Brutus and Cassius in the street. Brutus is afraid that their plot has been discovered, but Cassius can tell from Caesar's confidence that it hasn't. 'It's me or him,' Cassius says. 'If this fails, I'll kill myself.'

They join the others around Caesar. One of the plotters has been primed to whisk Antony out of the way. (Antony might cause trouble if he's there when the dirty deed is done.)

It's time for Caesar to hear people's requests. **Metellus Cimber** pleads for his brother, who has been thrown out of Rome. Caesar is high and mighty in his reply.

'Begging and pleading won't get you anywhere,' he says. 'If you don't stop grovelling, I'll kick you out, too.'

They all surround Caesar. Brutus speaks up for Metellus Cimber's brother, then Cassius joins in.

Caesar meanwhile is bragging about what an awesome bloke he is. He compares himself to the brightest star in the heavens, the only one that is not moving. He says he will not change his mind about Cimber's brother, and he mocks them for trying to make him do so.

Casca is the first to stab Caesar. '*Speak, hands for me!*' he shouts, as the blade goes in. Then the others plunge in their knives.

Brutus is the last to stab him. Caesar can't believe his friend would do this. '*Et tu, Brute?* What, even you, Brutus?' he gasps, as he sinks to the floor. It's all over very quickly. Caesar is dead.

There is confusion and celebration.
'*Liberty! Freedom! Tyranny is dead!*' shouts
Cinna. 'Run and tell everybody in the streets!'

Brutus reassures the crowd. 'Don't be
afraid. Caesar is the only one who had to
die. We won't harm anybody else.'

Then news comes that Antony has fled.
The conspirators think that's the last they'll
see of him.

Brutus gets them all to dip their hands in
Caesar's blood. They'll go to the market
place and show everyone their bloody
knives. They must persuade the crowds that
Caesar had to die.

Everyone is very upbeat. Cassius calls
out, '*Brutus shall lead; and we will grace his heels*
With the most boldest and best hearts of Rome.'

But before they leave, a servant arrives
from Antony. He makes a very grovelling
speech. He says that Antony will stick by
Brutus if Brutus will give him safe passage.

'*Mark Antony shall not love Caesar dead*

*So well as Brutus living; but will follow
The fortunes and affairs of noble Brutus.'*

Should Brutus believe him? Can he trust Antony? Cassius is not so sure, but Brutus promises that Antony will be safe. 'If he comes here, he will leave unharmed.'

The servant leaves to give Antony the news, and it isn't long before Antony himself arrives. When he sees Caesar's body, he asks to be put to death, too, next to Caesar.

'O Antony, don't beg us to kill you,' Brutus tells him. '*Our arms ... do receive you in*

With all kind love, good thoughts, and reverence.' Brutus wants to be friends with Antony.

Antony shakes hands with all of the conspirators, one by one. Then he turns again to the body of Caesar.

'*That I did love thee, Caesar, O, 'tis true ...* ' he sighs. Antony hopes the spirit of Caesar isn't upset if he makes friends with those who killed him. He tells the corpse how sorry he is.

Is Antony's friendship with the conspirators genuine? Or does he have a cunning plan?

Cassius asks Antony if he will be loyal to them.

'Of course I will,' says Antony, 'provided *that you shall give me reasons*

Why and wherein Caesar was dangerous.'

'Of course we had good reasons,' Brutus tells him.

Antony asks if he can bring Caesar's body to the marketplace and speak at his funeral.

'Of course,' says Brutus.

Cassius, as usual, isn't so sure. He pulls Brutus to one side. '*You know not what you do: do not consent*

That Antony speak in his funeral:

Know you how much the people may be moved

By that which he will utter?'

But Brutus insists. He'll speak first at the funeral and will tell the crowds the reasons for Caesar's death.

'Antony, you can speak at the funeral, but you will not blame us in your speech. You'll say good things about Caesar and you'll say you do it with our permission.'

'I don't like this plan,' Cassius whispers.

At last, Antony is left alone with Caesar's body. Now he can say what he is really thinking.

'*O, pardon me, thou bleeding piece of earth,*
That I am meek and gentle with these butchers!' He speaks with great feeling. 'Caesar, you were the noblest man that ever lived. Now civil war will paralyse all of Italy. Blood and destruction shall be so common that mothers will just smile when they see their infants cut to pieces by the hands of war. *Cry "Havoc," and let slip the dogs of war;*
That this foul deed shall smell above the earth
With carrion men, groaning for burial.'

OK. So now we know what Antony really thinks!

As he is speaking, a servant arrives, sent

by **Octavius Caesar**, Julius Caesar's adopted son. The servant has news that Octavius is near Rome. Antony sends the servant back with the news of Caesar's death. He adds, 'Tell Octavius that Rome isn't safe for him yet.'

At the Forum, Brutus and Cassius are getting ready to speak to the crowds. Cassius takes some people into the next street to explain to them why Caesar had to be murdered.

Most people stay to hear '*noble*' Brutus give his reasons. So Brutus climbs onto the platform and begins to speak.

First, he tells the crowd that he loved Caesar; nobody loved him more. So why did he help to kill him?

'*This is my answer: Not that I loved Caesar less, but that I loved Rome more.*'

He asks them, '*Had you rather Caesar were living and die all slaves, than that Caesar were dead, to live all free men?*' Caesar was killed because he had too much ambition. Brutus asks if he has offended anyone in the crowd.

'None,' they say.

As Brutus carries on speaking, Antony arrives with Caesar's body. Brutus makes a promise: 'I slew my best friend for the good of Rome, and *I have the same dagger for myself, when it shall please my country to need my death.*' Brutus killed Caesar because it was right for Rome; if Brutus's death is also right for Rome, then he will accept that.

Is this an omen of what's to come?

Everyone shouts their support for Brutus. He has the full support of the crowd.

'*Let him be Caesar!*' someone shouts. ['Caesar' is the name of Julius Caesar, but it is also the name given to the Emperor of Rome.]

Brutus thanks them, then asks them to hear Antony speak. People in the crowd agree to listen to Antony for Brutus's sake. Brutus leaves. (Bad move, Brutus!)

Now Antony is a clever man. He has promised not to say anything against the conspirators, but he has a way with words.

He begins, *'Friends, Romans, countrymen, lend me your ears;*

I come to bury Caesar, not to praise him.' He talks about Caesar, then says, *'Brutus says he was ambitious;*

And Brutus is an honourable man.' Antony repeats this three times, each time saying something good that Caesar had done, followed by, *'Brutus is an honourable man.'*

Antony does the emotional bit too: *'My heart is in the coffin there with Caesar,*

And I must pause till it come back to me.' Then he weeps.

People in the crowd begin to change their minds. *'Caesar has had great wrong,'* says one man. Others agree. They begin to think that what's to come might be worse than Caesar. Clever Antony! Brutus should have listened to Cassius.

Now for Antony's next move. 'I have

found Caesar's will,' he says. 'But I will not read it out to you.'

The crowd calls for him to read out the will, but Antony teases them. 'I must not read it,' he says. 'It's not right for you to know how much Caesar loved you.'

He has already got the crowd on his side. They start calling Brutus and the rest '*traitors*'.

But there is more. Crafty Antony shows them Caesar's body. '*If you have tears, prepare to shed them now,*' he says.

He points out each stab wound. 'Look, this is where Cassius stabbed him. Here is the wound that *the envious Casca* made. Through this hole the well-beloved Brutus stabbed him. *This was the most unkindest cut of all.*'

The crowd is eating out of his hands, ready to do anything for him. '*Revenge! About! Seek! Burn! Fire! Kill! Slay! Let not a traitor live!*' they shout.

Is that enough for Antony? Not likely!

'Good friends,' he says, 'don't let me stir you up into a sudden mutiny. The people that did this deed are wise and honourable. I'm not a great speaker, like Brutus, I'm just *a plain blunt man* who loved a friend.'

There's one final trick up Antony's sleeve. Now he reads Caesar's will to the crowd. 'To every Roman citizen, to every man, Caesar gives seventy-five drachmas. Plus, he's left you all his walks, his private gardens and his newly-planted orchards to enjoy.'

Antony is rubbing his hands in glee as the mutinous crowd rushes away to cremate Caesar's body and then burn '*the traitors' houses*'. He's turned the crowd with cunning skill – and now he'll just wait to watch what he knows will happen:

'*Now let it work. Mischief, thou art afoot,
Take thou what course thou wilt!*'

As he is revelling in his success, a messenger arrives to say that Octavius has arrived in Rome.

Cinna, the poet, is walking in another street in Rome when he meets some of the angry crowd. He is on his way to Caesar's funeral. They ask him who he is. He says his name is Cinna. 'Tear him to pieces,' shouts a man. 'He's a conspirator.'

They won't listen to his protests that he's innocent, that he's not *that* Cinna. They're so fired up they drag him away, eager for a lynching.

FOUR

Sometime later, Antony, Octavius and **Lepidus** are in a house in Rome. They're discussing which of the conspirators should die. Anyone who was connected to any of the conspirators is put on the list. They have to be ruthless; they have to remove anyone who might be against them.

Antony sends Lepidus to fetch Caesar's will. Antony wants to look at it, to work out how he can reduce the amount of money Caesar has left to the Roman people.

After Lepidus has gone, Antony talks to Octavius. He tells him that Lepidus is a pretty ordinary person, only fit to be sent on errands.

'Surely it's not right,' Antony tells Octavius, 'that, once we've split the world into three parts, Lepidus should be one of the three to share it.'

So Antony is not quite as noble as he appears!

Octavius tells Antony that Lepidus is *'a tried and valiant soldier.'*

'So is my horse, Octavius,' says Antony. Ouch!

They have heard that Cassius and Brutus are gathering their armies together, so Antony and Octavius head off to assemble their own armies.

The scene moves to Brutus's army's camp near Philippi, in Greece. Brutus arrives outside his tent with some friends and soldiers. He asks about Cassius and learns that he is close by with his own army.

Shortly afterwards, Cassius halts his army and comes to meet Brutus. Cassius is not happy. Straight away, he accuses Brutus. '*Most noble brother, you have done me wrong.*'

'Who, me?' says Brutus. 'What have I done?' But before Cassius can begin, Brutus stops him. 'Let's not argue in front of our armies.'

They send the soldiers out of earshot, then go into Brutus's tent, where Brutus promises to listen to Cassius.

Inside the tent, Cassius accuses Brutus of condemning one of his men who had taken bribes. Brutus hints that Cassius should be careful, as Brutus knows that Cassius too has taken bribes.

Cassius is angry and they have a blazing row. Brutus has had enough of Cassius's bad temper.

Then Cassius draws his dagger and asks Brutus to kill him. '*Strike, as thou didst at Caesar,* because I know that you loved him more than you love me.'

'Don't be an idiot,' says Brutus. 'Of course I love you. I just don't like you when you get angry.'

They make their peace with each other, but is there still a grudge between them?

Then Brutus tells Cassius that his (Brutus's) wife Portia is dead. She was missing Brutus, and was also worried about Antony's growing power. Losing her mind, she died a ghastly death: she '*swallow'd fire*'! (She probably swallowed hot coals.)

Brutus immediately puts any grief he has to the back of his mind: '*Speak no more of her,*' he tells Cassius.

They receive news that Antony and Octavius have put many senators to death. Now they've gathered massive troops together and have arrived at Philippi.

Cassius suggests that they wait for Antony and Octavius to come to them to fight. Brutus disagrees; he says that the other army could collect more men on the way.

'OK,' says Cassius. 'We'll go forward ourselves, and meet them at Philippi.'

But is Brutus the best judge of what to do? Is this a wise move?

The two men part for the night, friends again. Brutus tells his servants to get some sleep. Now he is alone.

Suddenly, the ghost of Caesar enters. Scary! The ghost tells Brutus it has come, *'To tell thee thou shalt see me at Philippi.'*

Then the ghost vanishes.

Is this a bad omen? Brutus thinks so. He wakes his servants and asks if they saw anything. No one did. Only Brutus has seen the ghost.

He sends a messenger to Cassius. 'Tell him to mobilise his forces first thing. I will follow.'

FIVE

On the plains of Philippi (the field of battle), Antony and Octavius are preparing their armies. They have heard that Brutus and Cassius are coming with their armies to meet them at Philippi.

A messenger tells them that the enemy is approaching. Antony and Octavius are planning their battle strategy when Brutus and Cassius arrive with their armies. (The theatre must have had a big stage to fit everybody on!)

The four leaders exchange insults. Antony is still very bitter. But actions are stronger than words, they say, so Antony and Octavius leave to make ready for the battle.

Brutus leaves Cassius for a moment and Cassius confides in a soldier. '**Messala**, today is my birthday.' He feels uneasy. He has seen strange omens. But Messala tells him not to worry.

When Brutus returns, Cassius asks him, *'Then, if we lose this battle*
You are contented to be led in triumph
Thorough the streets of Rome?'

'No,' says Brutus. 'I will not be taken to Rome as a captive. But today the work that we began on the ides of March must be finished.'

They prepare for battle.

On another part of the battlefield, Brutus sees danger from Octavius's army. He sends a message to his troops, telling them to fight on.

On the other side of the battlefield, Cassius is fighting Antony's army. He learns that Brutus has attacked too soon and his army is struggling against Octavius.

Then a soldier rushes towards Cassius. *'Mark Antony is in your tents, my lord*

Fly, therefore, noble Cassius, fly far off.'

Messengers arrive with more reports that the battle is lost.

Cassius is feeling desperate. He refuses to be taken alive, so he commands his servant to kill him:

'Now be a freeman: and with this good sword,

That ran through Caesar's bowels, search this bosom.'

The servant stabs Cassius, as ordered, then flees.

Cassius gasps, *'Caesar, thou art revenged, Even with the sword that kill'd thee.'*

Then Cassius dies.

As luck would have it, the tables have

turned and Brutus's army is now winning against Octavius – and Cassius's army is defeating Antony.

Then two soldiers find the body of Cassius. They are saddened, of course. While one soldier goes to tell Brutus the terrible news, the other soldier stabs himself with Cassius's sword and he too dies.

Brutus is devastated at the news of Cassius's death. '*O Julius Caesar, thou art mighty yet!*

Thy spirit walks abroad and turns our swords

In our own proper entrails.'

It is as if Caesar's spirit is making his enemies turn their swords on themselves.

Brutus says he will mourn Cassius later. Now he must fight on.

Antony's army soon seems to be overcoming Brutus's men. Antony wants to find Brutus and he sends soldiers to search for him.

In another part of the field, Brutus is cornered. He asks one of his soldiers to kill him, but the soldier is shocked: *'I'll rather kill myself.'* Brutus asks two more soldiers to kill him, but they too refuse.

Brutus tells another soldier that he has twice seen Caesar's ghost. *'I know my hour is come.* It's time for me to die.'

An alarm sounds. Things are coming to a head. For Brutus, there is no place to go. And he knows it.

So Brutus asks a soldier, *'Hold then my sword, and turn away thy face,*

While I do run upon it.'

Brutus runs onto his sword and dies. His dying words are, *'Caesar, now be still:*

I kill'd not thee with half so good a will.'

(Brutus is saying he killed Caesar half as willingly as he now kills himself.)

Then Octavius and Antony arrive and find Brutus's body. Both men are greatly saddened. They both speak well of Brutus.

Antony pays tribute. *'This was the noblest*

Roman of them all,' he says. 'All the other conspirators acted out of envy. Only Brutus acted honestly. His life was gentle, and the elements mixed so well *in him that Nature might stand up*

And say to all the world "This was a man!"'

Octavius promises to treat Brutus '*With all respect and rites of burial.*'

Then they go to celebrate their victory.

THE END

What's the play about?

This play is a historical drama based on events in the life of Julius Caesar. He was a very important Roman politician and a great military general. Nearly all the key characters in the play – including Brutus, Mark Antony and Cassius – were real people involved in the events of the time.

There *was* a plot to assassinate Caesar, and he was indeed assassinated on the ides of March. It also seems to be true that Caesar was surprised that his friend Brutus was part of the plot. But the words '*Et tu Brute?*' ('You too, Brutus?') were probably not said.

Rather than creating a new story, or *basing* his play upon historical events, Shakespeare has followed historical events very closely indeed, allowing him to explore a number of important themes (many of which Shakespeare revisited in other plays).

Despite the title of the play, Shakespeare's focus throughout is really on Brutus. In the play Brutus speaks four times as many lines as Julius Caesar. Remember also that Caesar actually dies quite early on in the play (at the beginning of Act Three).

A popular view of *Julius Caesar* is that the conspirators are motivated mostly by greed and envy, apart from Brutus, who is motivated by honour and patriotism. Similarly Antony is often regarded as acting out of selfless motives.

But a closer reading of the text shows that this view is too simplistic. All of the characters seem to be driven by a mix of motives, some good, some bad. In fact, it is difficult to find anybody in the play who is a true villain.

And that is the play's strength.

What are the main themes in the play?

Integrity – A central theme is how does a person manage to do the right thing – to do what they think is right – when faced with complex situations and conflicting pressures? Brutus struggles to decide whether to join the plot – Caesar is his friend, and murdering the leader of your country is not a decision taken lightly. He decides to join the plot because he thinks it is the right thing to do: Caesar must be stopped.

Brutus seems to act with the best intentions, but in the end he is defeated by Antony: not just by Antony's army, but also by Antony's much more practical approach to getting and keeping power. Antony falsely promises allegiance to Brutus and he gets the crowd on his side, but even then he is trying to go back on the promises he made. (For example, he wants to look at Caesar's will to try to find a way of reducing the amount they will need to pay out to the crowd.)

In the end it is the politics of power that win and it is a tragedy that Brutus's ideals are crushed. Was Brutus naïve? Or was Antony just better at playing politics than Brutus? Or was it a bit of both?

Honour – Ideas about honour are closely tied to ideas about integrity. At the end of the play, both Brutus and Cassius take their own lives; they think that, because they have been defeated in battle, this is the honourable thing to do.

At the end, Antony honours dead Brutus: '*This was the noblest Roman of them all.*' Is he recognising Brutus's honour and integrity? Or is he still just playing politics, wanting to get supporters of Brutus on his side?

Ambition and power – What price will

people pay to get power and to keep power? This is a universal theme, as true today as it was in Shakespeare's time or in ancient Rome.

In killing Caesar, the plotters accept that the death of their leader and friend is necessary to achieve what they want.

When Antony seeks to avenge Caesar's death, he says there will be civil war, with great suffering and bloodshed all round. He seems to believe that this is an acceptable price to pay to get the results he wants. (What results are those? Revenge? Justice? Or more power for himself?)

Many modern productions put the actors in modern clothing; in this way the play shows it is as relevant today as it has ever been.

Superstition and free will – In Shakespeare's time, many people believed that unusual natural events were omens, or signs, of important events in our lives.

In this play, for example, Caesar is warned (correctly) by a soothsayer to beware the ides of March. On the night before the assassination, there is a dramatic storm, with thunder and lightning. Towards the end of the play, Brutus believes that he is visited by Caesar's ghost.

What are the relationships between natural events and human actions? Can some people see into the future? If they can, does this mean that we do not have free will?

Persuasion – In this play, everybody seems to be trying to persuade somebody else about something. Cassius tries to persuade people to join the conspiracy. Brutus joins the plot, but he seems to need to persuade himself first that it's the right thing to do. Following Brutus's speech, Antony persuades the crowd to change their minds about Caesar's murder.

Even Caesar, in his own way, tries to persuade people to crown him (although this 'persuasion' includes refusing the offer of a crown three times first!)

Shakespeare's words

Julius Caesar includes a number of powerful and eloquent speeches. This should not be a surprise: ancient Rome was noted for its great orators, or speakers, and Shakespeare makes full use of the opportunity to put great words in their mouths.

As already noted, **persuasion** is an important part of this play. There are many great speeches where one character uses language to try to persuade others.

* The most famous speech in the play is Antony's speech to the crowd after Caesar's death:

    'Friends, Romans, countrymen, lend me your ears;

    I come to bury Caesar, not to praise him.

The evil that men do lives after them;'

The speech is a masterpiece of language and of manipulation. Antony has promised Brutus that he will not criticise the conspirators – yet he still manages to persuade the crowd to support him in avenging Caesar's death.

* Antony begins by stating the opposite of what he will do: '*I come to bury Caesar, not to praise him.*' It is a funeral speech, but Antony fully intends to praise Caesar – and to change the crowd's minds about their leader's death.

* Antony talks repeatedly about how Caesar was generous and admired, whilst at the same time admitting that Caesar was ambitious.

* He asks **rhetorical questions**. (These are questions he asks in order to make an impression on the crowd, rather than to get answers.)

* He describes the wounds in Caesar's body in detail, naming the conspirator responsible for each individual wound. The effect is to focus on the reality of the assassination and relate it directly to each conspirator.

* He uses Caesar's will to tempt the crowd. He speaks about the will, without revealing its contents, until the crowd insists that he read it to them.

* *Julius Caesar* is a play about politics, ambition and power, but the language is full of **images** of violence and war. There are references throughout to blood, death, sickness, nobility and honour.